S0-EKM-750

OUR VISION

CHRIST AND THE CHURCH

WITNESS LEE

Living Stream Ministry
Anaheim, California

First Edition, May 2002.

ISBN 0-7363-1836-4

Published by

Living Stream Ministry
2431 W. La Palma Ave., Anaheim, CA 92801 U.S.A.
P. O. Box 2121, Anaheim, CA 92814 U.S.A.

Printed in the United States of America

02 03 04 05 06 07 08 / 10 9 8 7 6 5 4 3 2 1

CONTENTS

PREFACE

This book contains notes of Brother Witness Lee's fellowship with various brothers and sisters. The first two chapters were spoken in Manila in June 1959, and the third chapter was given in Taipei in October of the same year. All these messages are urgently needed in the churches today. Hence, they have been collected and are now being published for the rich enjoyment of the saints everywhere.

Chapter One

THE VISION OF CHRIST AND THE CHURCH

Scripture Reading: Matt. 16:15-18; Eph. 5:32; Rom. 12:4-9; Col. 1:24-29

VISION AND SERVICE

The most important matter for a person who serves the Lord is that he must have a vision. Everyone who serves the Lord must be a person with a vision. Not all the brothers and sisters will have a vision directly from the Lord; some of them will see a vision indirectly through the help of others. At any rate, in principle, everyone must have a vision. If a person has a vision, his service is a service with a vision. The apostle Paul said that he was not disobedient to the heavenly vision (Acts 26:19). He served for his whole life according to the vision he had received.

Therefore, if we have a desire to serve, we must have a vision. We must ask the Lord to grant us a vision. Furthermore, I hope that we do not just receive trivial visions that are peripheral. Rather, we need to see the most central vision, the most fundamental vision, in God's purpose so that we may have a real understanding and seeing of the most basic and central matters concerning God's intention.

GOD'S CENTRAL VISION—CHRIST AND THE CHURCH

Now we would like to speak about God's central vision. This vision concerns the good pleasure of God's desire, the central purpose of God's plan in the universe.

If we carefully read through the Scriptures, we will see that God's focus in the universe, especially in the New Testament age of grace, is on Christ and the church. Recall that day in the district of Caesarea Philippi when the Lord asked the disciples, "Who do you say that I am?" (Matt. 16:15). At that time the Lord had already been with the disciples for a considerable length of time. The disciples had been under the Lord's leadership and had gained a considerable amount of knowledge concerning Him. Peter answered and said, "You are the Christ, the Son of the living God." Immediately the Lord answered and said to him, "Blessed are you, Simon Barjona, because flesh and blood has not revealed this to you, but My Father who is in the heavens" (vv. 16-17).

God revealed Christ to Peter, and this revelation was a vision. Then the Lord said to Peter that he is a stone (the Greek word for *Peter* means a "stone") and that upon this rock He would build His church (v. 18). Because Peter knew who Christ was, the Lord revealed the church to him.

Then in Ephesians 5, when referring to the fact that a husband shall be joined to his wife and the two shall be one flesh, the apostle said, "This mystery is great, but I speak with regard to Christ and the church" (vv. 31-32). In these two portions of the Word, which concern the Father's revelation and the mystery in the universe, Christ and the church are linked together. Therefore, Christ and the church are God's central intention, God's greatest delight in the universe. As those who serve the Lord, the central vision we should see is Christ and the church.

CHRIST BEING OUR LIFE

Christ to us is a matter of life. The Bible says that Christ is our life (Col. 3:4). Christ came to die for us on the cross; then in His resurrection He entered into the Holy Spirit. Christ redeemed us so that He could come into us to be our life. Christ was God incarnated to be mingled with man. The principle of Christ is the mingling of God and man, and this God who was mingled with man is in us to be our life. Hence, whenever Christ is mentioned, there is the thought of His being life to us. If we have a desire to serve God today, we must have a considerable amount of knowledge concerning this matter of Christ's being life to us. Instead of just listening to some messages about life, we must see the vision of Christ as life and live practically by Him as life.

A Thorough Consecration

If we desire to live practically by Christ as life, we must first consecrate ourselves. What is consecration? Consecration means that we hand ourselves over to Christ and let Him be our life. A consecrated person is a person who continually hands himself over to the Lord. Although we have our own will, we give it up and take Christ's will as our will. Although we have our own love, we give it up and take Christ's love as our love. In the same way, although we have our own thoughts and inclinations, we give them all up and take Christ's thoughts as our thoughts and Christ's inclinations as our inclinations. We must turn ourselves over to Christ completely and take Him into us to be our life. Although we have life and are living, we have given up our life and take Christ as our life instead.

Whether or not we can take Christ as our life depends on whether or not we are seriously willing to give everything of ourselves to Him. Only a person who gives himself completely to the Lord can be a person who truly knows Christ as life. Such a person is usually a very strong person. Those who are weak are not willing to consecrate, to hand over, themselves to the Lord in a serious way. Reading from the Old Testament through the New Testament, you can see that those who loved the Lord intensely were strong. People such as Samuel, Daniel, Peter, Paul, and the martyrs throughout the generations were all very strong. They handed themselves over completely and took Christ to be their life. To them this was not a doctrine; rather, they practically received Christ into their daily walk and life. Hence, they could say, "It is no longer I who live, but it is Christ who lives in me," and "For to me, to live is Christ" (Gal. 2:20; Phil. 1:21). Because they gave themselves up completely, they could practically experience Christ as their life.

A Renewed Love

This kind of consecration needs to be maintained by a

fresh love to the Lord. We need consecration, and we also need love. Furthermore, this love needs to be renewed daily, weekly, monthly, and yearly. We have to renew this love every morning. We have to renew this love on the first day of every week, that is, on the Lord's Day, we have to renew this love on the first day of the month, and we have to renew this love at the beginning of every year. Furthermore, we even have to renew this love in everything and in every situation. We should tell the Lord, "Lord, I love You. I want to be Your lover." By always renewing our love to the Lord in this way, we will be able to maintain our consecration to Him.

Fellowshipping and Inquiring

To experience Christ as life, in addition to consecrating ourselves and maintaining our consecration in love, we also need to have constant fellowship with the Lord, always waiting in His presence. We need to look to Him, inquire of Him, and take counsel with Him in our daily life concerning all matters, whether great or small. We have to always ask the Lord, "Lord, are You with me in all these things—in the way I speak, in the way I treat others, in the way I spend my money, and in the way I dress myself?" This is not to be religious or to keep certain regulations; rather, this is to allow Christ to be our life. When we fellowship with Christ and inquire of Him in this way, He will be our life practically in our daily walk. Therefore, we can see that Christ to us is a matter of life.

THE CHURCH BEING OUR LIVING

Then what is the church to us? The church to us is a matter of living. Our living includes not only our walk and conduct but also our work and service. Our visitations, our preaching of the word, and our various other services all constitute our living. With an actor, his acting on the stage is one thing, and his actual living off the stage is another thing. A disobedient son may act as a very obedient person on the stage, and his performance can be quite moving. Likewise, a person can act as a highly moral person on the stage, yet off the stage his living may be quite corrupt. This is to perform.

We are not like this. Our preaching of the word, our visitations, and our services should be our living. All the work and services in the church are our living. Our living is the church.

Not Being Independent

Why is it that our living is the church? It is because if we truly know Christ as our life and live by Him in everything, we will be built up with all the saints together in the Holy Spirit. At this stage, we will no longer be independent, nor will we even be able to be independent. We will not be able to work independently or even live independently. I must live in the church with the brothers and sisters, because the Christ in me is also in them. Christ is life to me as well as to the brothers and sisters. We all enjoy the same Christ as life. Christ lives in me, and He also lives in them. I live by Christ, and they also live by Christ. We all live by the same Christ. Therefore, we cannot be separated, nor can we live an independent life any longer. We can only live together. When Christ is lived out through us in this way, that is the church. When we have the church, we will no longer be independent.

In God's eyes the church life is worth much more than our individual life. Although we can pray by ourselves individually, we can enjoy the most crucial and best prayers when we pray together with the brothers and sisters, not when we pray by ourselves. Although we can worship individually, we enjoy more precious and higher worship when we worship together with the brothers and sisters. Likewise, the most effective gospel preaching is the gospel preaching by the whole church. We may say that all worthy services are services in the church.

Hence, our living, action, work, and service all should be in a builded condition and all should be in the church. This is not to say that we have an organization in which all of us are unified. Rather, this is to say that because we know the Christ who is life in us and because we love Him, consecrate ourselves and our everything to Him, have fellowship with Him, and live in Him, He spontaneously builds us up together. Therefore, the church is a corporate entity, a spiritual Body, formed by the building together of all the saved ones. Each one of us is just a member of the Body of Christ. As such, we cannot be detached from the Body, we cannot be Christians in an individual way, and we cannot serve the Lord independently.

Keeping the Order in the Body

As the Body, the church must be vertical instead of only being horizontal. If this is the case, there will be order in the church. In the church we cannot be independent, and we also cannot stay away from the order. Whenever we leave the order, we leave the Body. Whenever we lose the proper order, our fellowship with the Body is interrupted. Losing the proper order indicates that we are still living an independent life and have stopped living the church life. This also means that we have stopped taking Christ as our life. Whenever we let Christ be our life, our living will surely be the church, and spontaneously we will not be able to be independent, we will keep the order, and we will have the coordination. When we know the order in the Body and accept God's arrangement, we will know God's authority in the church.

TAKING THE VISION OF CHRIST AND THE CHURCH AS THE GOAL OF OUR SERVICE

The vision of Christ and the church is related not only to our personal growth in life but also to the building up of the church on earth. When we experience Christ as life, we can then have the growth in life. When we live the church life, the church can then be built up. Hence, each of us who serve the Lord must see the vision of Christ and the church. We need to see and live in such a vision. This vision should also become the goal of our service. It should be like a brightly shining lamp, and we should walk in its light. If we are serving the children in the church, we must help them to know Christ in their youth and to become materials for the building of the church, so that one day they too will be built up together. If we are serving the young people, then by the wisdom given to us by God, we should help them to receive Christ, so that they may become useful materials in the church to be the future deacons, elders, and evangelists. If we have seen the vision of

Christ and the church, the goal of all of our service will be to help others receive Christ as life, so that they may become proper materials who are built up in the church. In all of our services, we should exercise all wisdom to help people to gain Christ as life, so that they may become materials for the building and be built up as the spiritual house of God. Brothers and sisters, this is our vision.

TAKING CHRIST AS LIFE AND ENTERING INTO THE BODY OF CHRIST

We know that the one book in the Scriptures which most clearly depicts the levels of our spiritual life is the book of Romans. This book tells us clearly the stages of the believer's spiritual journey, spiritual experience, before God. From chapter one through the first half of chapter three Romans shows us that all the people in the world are sinners who do not know God and who are under God's condemnation. From the second half of chapter three through chapter four it shows us that by believing and receiving Christ's redemption, sinners are justified and accepted by God and thereby reconciled to God. In chapter five it tells us that those who have been redeemed and justified by God were formerly in Adam and had inherited sin and death. Chapter six tells us that through faith and baptism we are united with Christ, that we are in Christ, and that we have received Christ's death and resurrection. Through Christ's death we have been delivered from the sin in Adam, and through Christ's resurrection we have been delivered from the death in Adam. Chapter seven tells us that in our experience we know the old creation, in our practical daily life we know the impotence of our flesh, and as a result we realize that the old creation and our flesh are incurable. The first half of chapter eight tells us that if we live by the law of the Spirit of life and walk according to the spirit, we are those who live in the Holy Spirit. The second half of chapter eight tells us that we are being conformed to the image of God's Son, not only through the work of the Spirit of God within us but also through the working together of all things outside of us arranged by God. Therefore, when we arrive at chapter eight, inwardly we are filled with the

Holy Spirit, and outwardly we have been broken by the environment; our entire being is conformed to the image of Christ. At this point we have completely received Christ as our life and are also completely living in Christ. Chapters nine through eleven are a parenthetical word. Chapter twelve, continuing chapter eight, tells us that we have to consecrate ourselves to God in a practical way by presenting our bodies a living sacrifice to God. We live in our body, so we have to present our body to have a practical consecration. Chapter twelve goes on to say that we are one Body in Christ, and individually we are members one of another. When we present our bodies, the Body of Christ is perfected and manifested.

In Romans 12 there are two bodies: our body and the Body of Christ. If we hold on to our body, the Body of Christ cannot be perfected. If we want to build up the Body of Christ, we must present our body. The question is, do we intend to keep our own body, or do we desire to build up the Body of Christ? If we hold on to our own body, there cannot be the Body of Christ. If we hold on to our self, there cannot be the church. To have the church, we must let go of our self. We must present our body a living sacrifice. Only then can we become members of the Body of Christ in practicality, and only then will gifts and functions be manifested in us.

Some have been saved for many years, yet there is no function or gift manifested in them. This is because they are not willing to present their bodies; they are not willing to live in the Body of Christ. Romans 12 shows us that even things in our daily life, such as showing mercy and loving the brothers, are gifts. You may not be able to preach the word, and you may not appear to know much, but if you are considerate toward others and have a heart to love the brothers, these are also gifts. Romans 12 joins the spiritual life and spiritual gifts together. The apostle mentions various gifts, including prophesying as prophets, serving as deacons, teaching, exhorting, giving, leading, showing mercy, and loving the brothers. He tells us that all these are gifts. Not only prophesying, teaching, and leading are gifts, but even giving, showing mercy, and loving the brothers are gifts. All these are spiritual gifts as well as aspects of the spiritual living. The

Spirit shows us here that when we present our bodies, the result is that all these gifts, functions, will be manifested in the Body of Christ, which is the church, for the building up of the Body of Christ.

SUFFERING ON BEHALF OF THE BODY OF CHRIST AND BUILDING UP THE BODY OF CHRIST

In Colossians 1 the apostle Paul said that he suffered for the Body of Christ to fill up that which is lacking of the afflictions of Christ. We have to know that Christ underwent two kinds of suffering. The first kind of suffering is the suffering for substitution in which He was judged and stricken by God for our sins. None of us can have any share in this kind of suffering. He alone went through this kind of suffering for us. The second kind of suffering is the suffering for germination. This kind of suffering can be likened to a grain of wheat falling into the earth and dying and thereby bringing forth many grains. This kind of suffering is for the releasing and imparting of life to us for the producing of the church. Christ has not yet completed this aspect of His suffering; there is still a lack. This is what Paul referred to as "that which is lacking of the afflictions of Christ" (v. 24). This kind of affliction needs to be filled up by all the lovers of the Lord throughout the ages. The three thousand and the five thousand who were saved in the early days of the church could not have been saved without the sufferings experienced by the first group of apostles. The early churches could not come into existence without the sufferings experienced by Paul and his co-workers. Likewise, if we do not undergo sufferings, we cannot cause others to receive Christ as life, bear many grains, or gain many members for the building up of the Body of Christ. Therefore, we who serve the Lord should fill up that which is lacking of the afflictions of Christ for His Body.

The apostle Paul said that his sufferings were for the church and his serving as a minister was also for the church. He served the Lord as a minister of the church to complete the word of God, which was the mystery hidden from the ages and from the generations, which is Christ in us, the hope of glory. Therefore, Paul preached Christ, and the issue was the church. His work was to release Christ for the building up of the church. He ministered Christ to every man in all wisdom that he might present every man full-grown in Christ for the building up of the Body of Christ, which is the church (vv. 25-29). Therefore, the work of the apostle was, on the one hand, for people to receive Christ as their life, and on the other hand, for people to take the church as their living. This should also be our service today. In all of our service in the church, we should bring Christ to people that they may receive Him and be built up in the church.

THE REQUIREMENTS OF THE VISION

If we desire to serve the Lord according to this vision, we must be prepared to satisfy the requirements of this vision. A person who serves according to this vision must be willing to pay a price and to suffer. It is not enough to just pay a price; we must also accept sufferings. Hence, the apostle said that there is the need to fill up that which is lacking of the afflictions of Christ. If you truly live by Christ and serve God by Christ, and if you truly desire to admonish others in all wisdom for them to gain Christ and be built up into the Body of Christ, then you must be ready to pay a price and also to undergo sufferings. Only those who are willing to pay a great price and to undergo sufferings can walk on the way of service.

Please remember, however, that the price we pay will enable us to gain the glorious Christ and the glorious church, and the sufferings we undergo are for us to gain the glorious Christ and the glorious church. Compared to the glory which will be manifested to us in the future, the momentary lightess of affliction means nothing. Therefore, we should not hesitate from going forward, considering the price to be too great and the afflictions too heavy. We have to see what we will gain for the price we pay and the afflictions we experience. Praise God, what we get instead is a priceless treasure.

If we see this vision, we will know what race we are running, what work we are doing, and whom we are serving. If we have seen this vision, no amount of opposition and hardship will be able to cause us to be shaken or to be disobedient. This is because this vision is glorious and has eternal worth.

PURSUING TO KNOW CHRIST AND THE CHURCH

Finally, we need to pursue to know Christ, and we also need to pursue to know the church. Christ is our life, and the church is our living. For us to live is Christ, and what we live out is the church. When Christ grows in us, the church is built up. If we truly let Christ live in us, He will not allow us to be independent, nor will He allow us to always be horizontal, without any order and without any authority. That the church is our living is seen clearly in two matters: first, that the members cannot be independent but are coordinated with one another; second, that there cannot be the absence of order and authority. This is just like our body—no member is independent; instead, every member is coordinated with other members. Furthermore, every member has its order, and with this order there is authority. To cease from being independent is to be coordinated, and to keep the order is to be vertical. This is the church life.

May the Lord grant every one of us to have this glorious vision of Christ and the church.

Chapter Two

TAKING CHRIST AS OUR LIFE AND THE CHURCH AS OUR LIVING

Scripture Reading: Phil. 4:13; John 14:19; 6:57, 63; Gal. 2:20; Rom. 12:5-8; 1 Cor. 12:12, 14-16; Eph. 4:13; 1 Cor. 10:17

Philippians 4:13 says, "I am able to do all things in Him who empowers me." This word was spoken by the apostle Paul. He said this to show us that in his living and in his work he did not do anything in himself, by his own strength, or by his own life. He did everything in Christ who empowered him. This word shows us that he took Christ as life.

John 14:19 says, "Because I live, you also shall live." In saying "I live," the Lord referred to His living after His resurrection. The Lord was put to death, yet He was resurrected, so He still lives. After His resurrection, He does not live in Himself alone, but He causes all who belong to Him to live also. Hence, the Lord said, "Because I live, you also shall live." This word of the Lord implies also that the reason we live is because He not only lives, but because He lives in us. Because the Lord lives in us, we also shall live.

John 6:57 says, "As the living Father has sent Me and I live because of the Father, so He who eats Me, he also shall live because of Me." This word means that just as the Lord did not live by Himself but by the Father because the Father lived in Him, so we who eat the Lord, who receive Him into us as food, also live because of Him.

Verse 63 continues, "It is the Spirit who gives life; the flesh profits nothing; the words which I have spoken to you are spirit and are life."

These three verses in John—14:19, 6:57, and 6:63—mention *live* and *life*. Galatians 2:20 also mentions *live* and *lives*. This verse says, "I am crucified with Christ; and it is no longer I who live, but it is Christ who lives in me." I like to read these four passages together. The first passage says, "Because I live, you also shall live." The second passage says, "He who eats Me, he also shall live because of Me." The third passage says, "It is the Spirit who gives life;...the words which I have spoken to you are spirit and are life." And the last passage says, "It is no longer I who live, but it is Christ who lives in me." These verses show how Christ is life to us.

In the previous message we said that a person who serves the Lord must see the central vision of God in the universe—Christ and the church. This central vision in the universe is the great mystery of God. If we have truly seen this central vision—Christ and the church—our entire being will be under its direction and control. This vision must not be just a doctrine to us; it must be a reality in our living. If we have such a vision, it will not be possible for us to live by ourselves apart from Christ, and it will also not be possible for us to live independently apart from the church. The result of seeing this vision is that Christ becomes our life and the church becomes our living.

HOW TO TAKE CHRIST AS OUR LIFE

Enjoying the Lord by Prayer and Reading the Word

To take Christ as our life is to live by Christ. The verses listed above show us how we can live by Christ. In John 14 the Lord said that because He lives, we also will live. This word of the Lord indicates that after His resurrection, we would be able to take Him as our life and thereby live by Him and because of Him. How can this be? In John 6 the Lord pointed out that he who eats Him shall live because of Him. This means that if we want to live because of Him, we need to receive Him into us by eating Him. How can we receive Him into us? When the Jews heard the Lord's word at that time, they also asked the same question. They asked, "How can this man give us His flesh to eat?" (v. 52). What the Lord said in verse 63 was the answer. He said, "It is the Spirit who gives life;...the words which I have spoken to you are spirit and are life." We all know that the Lord is the Spirit. Therefore, it is the Lord Himself who gives us life and causes us to live. Today the Lord is living in us as the Spirit. Hence, if we want to the eat the Lord, we must learn to turn to our spirit to eat Him. This is because the Lord is the Spirit, the Spirit gives us life and enables us to live, and the Spirit is in our spirit. Therefore, in everything we need to learn to turn to our spirit to touch and contact the Spirit of the Lord. In this way we will receive the supply from the Lord and thus live by Him.

The Lord also said that His words are spirit. We know the Lord Himself is the living Word. Hence, to eat the Lord, there is not only the matter of the Spirit but also the matter of the word. In other words, the Lord is the Spirit, and He is also the word. The Lord is in the Spirit and in the word. Thus, in order to receive, to obtain, the Lord, we have to contact His Spirit and His word. It is for this reason that we have to pray and also to read the Scriptures. To pray is to contact the Spirit, and to read the Scriptures is to touch the word. We pray so that we can touch the Spirit in our spirit and thereby receive the Lord Himself. We read the Scriptures so that we can touch the Lord's word and thereby receive the Lord Himself. Today our Lord is in the Spirit and in the word as well. Therefore, our contacting Him, touching Him, obtaining Him, and eating Him all depend on these two aspects. On the one hand, we need to turn to our spirit to touch the Spirit; on the other hand, we need to come to the Scriptures to touch the word. If we learn to constantly touch the Spirit in our spirit and touch the word in the Scriptures, we will constantly eat and drink the Lord and thereby receive and gain the Lord so that we can live by Him and because of Him.

Denying Ourselves and Not Living by Ourselves

If we want to take Christ as our life and live by Him, we also need to see that "I am crucified with Christ; and it is no longer I who live, but it is Christ who lives in me," as the apostle said in Galatians 2. Whereas the three verses we quoted from the Gospel of John all focus on how we can eat and drink the Lord to receive His supply, this verse in Galatians shows that we also need to go on to experience the co-death of the cross and to reject our own life. In order to experience Christ as our life, on the positive side, we need to absorb and enjoy the Lord and thereby live by Him; on the negative side, we need to see that we have to be put to death on the cross so that we will continually reject ourselves, deny ourselves, and not live by ourselves. Both sides are necessary.

Our emotions, preferences, opinions, ideas, insight, intelligence, ability, and capability are all our self, our natural life. To not live by ourselves is to not live by all these things of our natural life. Hence, in everything that we do in our daily life, we must deny all these natural things and not live by them. This is a serious lesson for every one of us.

We should learn this lesson not only in our daily life but even more in our work for the Lord and in our service in the church. Whether in ministering the word from the podium or in visiting people, we must learn the lesson according to this principle. For example, when you are going to give a message from the podium, you must immediately and seriously say to yourself, "I must not speak according to my preference, thoughts, opinions, insight, ideas, knowledge, eloquence, or boldness. I must speak only according to the Lord whom I have touched in spirit and in the word." After you have such a strict dealing, when you stand on the platform, you will be able to completely reject all that is natural. You will also be able to turn to your spirit to touch the Lord as the Spirit and to turn to the Scriptures to touch the Lord as the word. In this way while you are standing on the platform to release a message, you will not be doing so by yourself but by the Lord, that is, by taking the Lord as life. The principle is the same when you go to visit people. Whenever you go to visit people, you should always come back to your spirit and to the word to touch, to contact, the Lord. This is a serious lesson. Only those who have learned this lesson can have the experience of taking the Lord as life and living by Him.

THE ISSUE OF TAKING CHRIST AS LIFE—BEING BUILT TOGETHER AS THE CHURCH

Brothers and sisters, if we take the Lord as life and live by Him, the result will be that we will be built by the Lord to be His church. It is not doctrine that builds us together. Doctrines cannot cause us to be built up together as the church. If we truly desire to be built up as the church, we must take the Lord as life and live by Him. If we have truly learned this lesson in a serious way, living not by ourselves but by the Lord and taking not ourselves but the Lord as life, then spontaneously we will be built together with all the saints to be the Lord's church. This is why we say that the church is our living. Such a living is the issue of Christ's being lived out of us. Such a living is altogether the result of our living by Christ, taking Christ as our life, and allowing Christ to live in us.

Therefore, the basic lesson we have to learn is to strictly deny ourselves and live by Christ. When you take Christ as life, allow Christ to live in you, and allow Him to live out through you, the issue will be the church. When you allow Christ to live out through you, this is the building, the coordination. Anyone who takes Christ as life and lives by Him will not be individualistic but in coordination, and he will not only be horizontal but vertical. When we live in this way, our living is the church.

Therefore, if we want to know whether a person is taking Christ as life and whether he is living by Christ, we just have to see whether or not the church is the issue of his living. If in his living and work he is not coordinated with the brothers and sisters but rather is individualistic, this is proof that he is not living by Christ and not taking Christ as his life. If you live by Christ and take Christ as life, the result will be that you will be coordinated with the brothers and sisters and that you will not be able to be independent. Furthermore, the relationship between you and the brothers and sisters will not only be horizontal but vertical, having the authority and the order.

Hence, in the Epistles there are many verses telling us how the apostles took Christ as their life and how they lived by Christ. There are also many verses telling us how they lived in the Body. What they lived out was the Body of Christ and the house of God. They were coordinated together in one Body and built up into one dwelling place. Therefore, they were not horizontal but vertical, not individualistic but coordinated.

Being Members One of Another to Become One Body

Romans 12:5 says that we are one Body in Christ and individually members one of another. Being members one of another is the living of the church. In such a living, there are some who teach, some who exhort, some who lead, some who serve, some who show mercy, and some who give. Whatever you do, however, you have to be coordinated with the brothers and sisters as members one with another.

In the previous message we said that Romans 12 is a continuation of Romans 8. It is only by passing through the experience of Romans 8 and living absolutely according to the spirit that a person can come to Romans 12 to be a member of the Body of Christ. Therefore, this also shows us that the church life is based upon our experience of taking Christ as life. If we take Christ as our life, living by Christ and allowing Christ to live out of us, the issue will definitely be a living in which we are members one of another.

The living referred to in Romans 12 is altogether a living of the brothers' and sisters' experience of being members one of another as one Body. Whether or not this one Body can be realized, whether or not it can be practical, and whether or not it can manifest its functions altogether depend upon our being members one of another. If the brothers' and sisters' experience of being members one of another is insufficient, improper, or problematic, then the Body cannot be realized and the functions of the Body cannot be manifested. The reason for this insufficiency is that the brothers and sisters do not adequately take Christ as life or live by Christ. If we still live in ourselves and by ourselves, there is no way for us to be joined together.

It Being Impossible for the Members to Be Independent

Since we live by Christ and thereby have the church life, we cannot be separated from one another and cannot be independent. First Corinthians 12 tells us that the eye cannot say to the hand, "I have no need of you," nor the head to the feet, "I have no need of you" (v. 21). In the church today we often quote these verses, yet in our heart we still may say, "I can do everything by myself; I do not need you." This shows that we are not taking Christ as life nor living out the church life. If our life is not Christ, then our living is not the church. If I live in Christ and take Christ as my life, I cannot help but live out the church life, and I cannot help but say to the brothers and sisters, "I need you." I will surely say that I need all the brothers and sisters. I am just an eye, so I need the ears, the nose, the mouth, the hands, and the feet. I need every brother and every sister, and they all need me too. I know that just as I cannot live apart from the Lord, so also I cannot live apart from the brothers and sisters. If as a member I leave the Head, I will become a detached member, a dead member. Likewise, if as a member I leave the Body, I will also become a detached member, a dead member. Christ is my life, and the life of Christ is a corporate life. He came not to be life to a single member, to an individual, but to be life to the Body. Therefore, I cannot take Him as life nor live by Him independently and not live in the Body. I cannot live only an individual member's life and not the Body life. If I take Christ as life and live by Him, what is lived out will be the church.

Do we actually have the church as our living? This is a real test. Many times we think that we are not wrong, but we realize that we are individualistic. Although we are not wrong, we are in ourselves—we neither live by Christ nor live in the church. The reason we are individualistic, acting as if we do not need the brothers and sisters, is that we feel that we are quite right and quite good. The result is that we are very individualistic. We have individuals but not the church. We do not have the church as our living, because we do not have Christ as our life. He who does not take Christ as life cannot live out the church life. That kind of living is not a coordinated church but an independent individual.

Becoming a Full-grown Man

The apostle Paul shows us in Ephesians 4 that when Christ lives and grows in us, eventually we will become a full-grown man (v. 13). The original text of this portion of the Scriptures does not refer to many full-grown men but to one full-grown man. We think that as we are in Christ individually and Christ is in us individually, gradually each one of us will become a full-grown person. You become a full-grown person, he becomes a full-grown person, and I also become a full-grown person. There is not such a thing. The apostle said that we all become a full-grown man. Therefore, if we truly have grown up, although we are many, we become one man. This one man is a great man of mystery, which is Christ and the church.

One Bread and One Body

Perhaps some will ask, "In John 12 did the Lord Jesus not say that if a grain of wheat falls into the ground and dies, it will bear many grains? Are these many grains not individual grains?" Please do not forget, however, that when we come to 1 Corinthians 10, there it tells us that "there is one bread," and that "we who are many are one Body" (v. 17). Previously there were many grains, but now these grains have become one bread. In other words, every one of the grains has to be ground; there is not one grain that is preserved whole. The grains are not only ground to powder but also blended as one dough and made into one bread. Hence, although individual grains were produced, eventually they become one bread. Therefore, although we are many, we are one bread, one Body.

This is Christ in us as our life and the church outside of us as our living. We cannot look at only one aspect. We cannot say, "As long as I stay away from sin, do not love the world, and act according to the will of the Lord in all things, that is good enough." Neither can we say, "As long as I live in the presence of God every day, and as long as everything I do is spiritual and pleasing to God, that is enough." We cannot look at just this one aspect. We still have to ask whether what we live out is one bread and whether it is one Body. Do we live out the church? Or do we live out our individualism—our individual victory, individual spirituality, and individual holiness? Are we members one of another with the brothers and sisters to the extent that we cannot live without one another? Or do we say in our heart to the brothers and sisters, "I do not need you"? If we feel that we cannot live without the brothers and sisters, that we need the brothers and sisters, then our living is the church. If I am an eye, then I need the feet, the hands, the ears, and the mouth. I need every part of the body. This is a builded situation. This is oneness, and this is harmony. This is what it means for us all to arrive at a full-grown man.

We often say that we all are *like* one man, but this is not enough. We should say that we all *are* one. Do we have one thousand brothers and sisters? These one thousand brothers and sisters are just one. Do we have two thousand brothers and sisters? These two thousand brothers and sisters are still one. Regardless of how many brothers and sisters there are, they are just one. If we all live by Christ and allow Christ to grow in us, the result will be that we all will become a full-grown man. This man is the church.

THE APPLICATION OF THIS VISION

Now we need to apply these words to ourselves. Please consider: How much of the element of coordination do we have among us? What is the degree of coordination among us? Or we may ask, How much of the element of the church life do we have in us? And how high is the degree? I believe that by asking ourselves in this way, immediately we will discover that although it seems that we are not wrong and we love the Lord very much, the weight of the church life is very light and the measure is very little. In fact, there is almost no measure. It seems that basically we do not know what a coordinated life is, what the church life is, and what the Body life is. Since we do not know these matters, we do not know what authority and order are. This is why we are poor, weak, dull, and stale. Although I dare not say that we are in darkness, I do dare to say we are not bright; instead, we are dim within, having shadows and veils. We lack power in our prayer, in our ministering of the word, and in our preaching of the gospel. Furthermore, our meetings are neither fresh nor living. People cannot sense the Lord's presence when they come into our meetings. All these conditions show that we lack Christ as our life and the church as our living. We do not have enough Christ as life, so we do not adequately have the church as our living. The reason for this is that we always remain in ourselves and always try to preserve our wholeness, being unwilling to be broken. We always try to keep ourselves as a grain of wheat and are not willing to be ground. Hence, we cannot get along with others, be in coordination with others, and be built up together with others.

Brothers and sisters, the vision concerning Christ and the church is not a doctrine; rather, it is God's central purpose in the universe. By His mercy may all of us who serve the Lord see this vision that in all things we may take Christ as life and live by Christ, so that the church can become our living and our testimony.

CHAPTER THREE

BEING TESTED, RESTRICTED, AND PROTECTED BY THE VISION OF CHRIST AND THE CHURCH

Scripture Reading: Eph. 5:32

CHRIST AND THE CHURCH BEING A GREAT MYSTERY IN THE UNIVERSE

Ephesians 5:32, a simple verse from the Scriptures, shows us that there is a great mystery in the universe—Christ and the church. In the Bible a number of mysteries are mentioned, but only this mystery, the mystery of Christ and the church, is a great mystery. First Timothy 3:16 says, "Confessedly, great is the mystery of godliness: He who was manifested in the flesh." This mystery refers to Christ, on the one hand, and to the church, on the other. Therefore, we can clearly and definitely say that Christ and the church are a great mystery. Although the Bible says that the mystery of God is Christ and that the mystery of Christ is the church, only when Christ and the church are mentioned together does the Bible say that this is a great mystery. We can say that if there were only Christ and not the church, the mystery would not be complete, and if there were only the church and not Christ, the mystery would not be possible. Therefore, this mystery must be constituted with both Christ and the church.

First let us see what a mystery is. According to common understanding, a mystery is something hidden and generally unknown to people. The meaning of the mystery mentioned in the Bible, however, goes beyond this. Strictly speaking, in the Bible a mystery not only refers to things that are incomprehensible and unknown to men but also to things that are hidden in God's heart.

For example, the universe with all the things created by God is very evident and therefore not a mystery. However, the purpose of God's creation of the universe is a mystery. All the people in the world have seen the God-created universe, but from the ancient days to the present time, very few have been able to fathom the purpose of God's creation. This is because the purpose for the creation of the universe was hidden in God's heart. It is nearly impossible for man to touch God's purpose, God's plan, which is hidden in His heart. Hence, it is a mystery. This is the principle concerning mysteries mentioned in the Bible.

Not only the purpose of God's creation is a mystery to the world, but even the church and the saints are a mystery to the world. Today people see that there are Christians and there is the church, but very few know why there are Christians and why there is the church. The unbelievers do not know this, and even many of those who serve and work for the Lord do not necessarily understand this, because this is also a mystery.

The church is something hidden in God's heart. Unless God reveals the mystery hidden in His heart concerning the church, we, like others, cannot know what the church is all about. We may preach the gospel fervently and serve the Lord diligently, but it is quite possible that we do not have any idea concerning what God intends to have in the universe. Hence, we all need to see a vision. The central vision God wants us to see in this age is the vision concerning Christ and the church.

Knowing Christ and the Church Being the Key to Knowing the Bible

Today many people pursue to understand the Bible. We know, however, that a person cannot understand the Bible unless he knows Christ. Likewise, a person cannot understand the Bible unless he knows the church. Strictly speaking, we should not pursue to understand and know the Bible; rather, we should pursue to know Christ and His church. The purpose of our knowing the Bible is that through it we may know Christ and the church. God gave us the Bible not merely for us to understand some truths in letter. God's purpose in giving us the Bible is that through His Word we may know the mystery which has been revealed—Christ and the church. Therefore, unless we have seen the vision of this mystery and thereby know Christ and the church, we cannot understand the Bible.

Pursuing to Know Christ and the Church

Hence, I would like to insert a few words here. Because we are touching Christ and the church, the subject of our fellowship, the center of our pursuit, and the content of our conversation are not just some biblical truths. What we treasure, pursue, and fellowship about is nothing other than Christ and the church. Christ and the church are too great! From the Word of God we can see that in Christ all the fullness of the Godhead dwells bodily (Col. 2:9). God puts everything that He is and has into Christ in order that Christ may come into us to be our everything. Hence, Ephesians 3 says that when Christ dwells in us and is touched and experienced by us, the result is that we will be filled unto all the fullness of God (vv. 17-19). Therefore, not only Christ is full, but the church is full. What we are endeavoring to pursue is to know Christ and the church.

KNOWING CHRIST AS LIFE

We should pursue to know how Christ, in whom is all the fullness of the Godhead, comes into us to be our life. Our pursuit today should not be concerned with how to be fervent, how to do good, or how to be determined; it should be concerned with how to know more about Christ being our life. We must be able to differentiate between our zeal and Christ, between our goodness and Christ, between our love and Christ. Many times when we see a brother who is zealous, well-behaved, and full of love, we think that such zeal, goodness, and love are what God wants. This view is quite problematic. We have to see that what God wants us to know, pursue, and live out is not any of these things but rather Christ Himself.

Living Out Christ through the Cross

We must pass through the cross to live out Christ. If we want to have Christ as our life and to have Him live out of us, we have no other alternative but to pass through the cross. To live out our zeal and our love, however, we do not have to go through the cross; we can live them out simply by our natural life. These things are natural and human; they are not Christ. The only way for a person to live out Christ is to go through the cross.

There is absolutely no room at the cross for our natural life. We have often discussed the matter of our natural life. We need to know, however, that only when a person has passed through the cross and allowed Christ to be his life, can he truly be one who knows the natural life. These two, our natural life and Christ as life, cannot exist together at the same time. We must see that the cross has terminated our natural life, on the one hand, and released Christ as our life, on the other. Whenever we live by our natural life, Christ's life is bound. Whenever we experience the cross, our natural life is eliminated and Christ's life is released.

Learning to Take Christ as Life in All Things

Therefore, we should not pay attention to such things as how to improve ourselves and how to do more good deeds and be more zealous. Rather, we should pay attention to asking ourselves in everything we do whether what we are doing is of Christ or of our natural life, whether we are living by Christ or by ourselves. We need to take heed to this way in spiritual things and also in the small things in our daily life. Even when we come to read the Word, we should ask ourselves, "Are the things that I am receiving from the Word causing the growth of Christ's life in me, or are they nourishing my natural life?" This is a solemn question. It is the case that with some brothers and sisters, their natural life becomes more prevailing even through their reading of the Word. They often have and hold strongly to their views concerning biblical truths. When they meet others who have opposite views, they engage them in strong debates and even quarrel with them. When you contact these ones, you cannot sense that Christ is life to them to any significant extent. Therefore, even in the matter of reading the Bible we need to go through the cross.

Not Contacting the Tree of the Knowledge of Good and Evil but the Tree of Life

In the beginning in the garden of Eden there were two trees: the tree of life and the tree of the knowledge of good and evil. In every matter there are also these two trees. In our Christian life we have the possibility of contacting either the tree of life or the tree of the knowledge of good and evil. Even while we are fellowshipping and talking with others about the things of the Bible, there is the possibility of contacting the tree of the knowledge of good and evil. Therefore, we have to beware of the stratagems of the evil one. He exploits every crack or loophole he can find. He even tries to sneak into the mutual fellowship of the believers so that unconsciously they are distracted from life and end up touching the things that are outside of life.

Brothers and sisters, the great mystery in God's heart is Christ and the church. If we have seen this vision, we will not pay attention to or pursue anything outside of Christ and the church. Then we will always be preserved. We will say only this much concerning Christ as our life.

PURSUING TO LIVE OUT THE CHURCH LIFE

Now let us consider the matter of the church. We have said many times that Christ is our life and that the church is our living. The more we know God's heart and the more we have His vision, the more thoroughly we will know that God's intention is for Christ to be our life inwardly and for us to live out the church outwardly. These two matters are clearly revealed in the Epistles written by the apostles. For example, chapter three of Colossians, a book on Christ as the Head of the church, has the phrase "Christ our life" (v. 4a). This shows us that the reason Christ can be the Head to the church is that He is our life. Ephesians, on the other hand, is a book on the church as the Body of Christ. Hence, in the entire book there is great stress on the various aspects of the Body life. We know that a person's living is altogether connected to his body. Without a body, a person does not have a living. This is also the case with Christ. How can Christ live Himself out? It is through His Body, which is the church. Christ as the Head is our life, and the church as the Body is our living.

Christians in general usually consider that the Christian life is to live out human virtues such as humility, patience, and love, but this is not what the Bible tells us. It is true that Ephesians 4:2-3 says, "With all lowliness and meekness, with long-suffering, bearing one another in love, being diligent to keep the oneness of the Spirit in the uniting bond of peace." Yet verse 4 also says, "One Body and one Spirit." Here we see clearly that the reason God wants us to be lowly and meek is that we may live out the Body.

How regrettable it is that although many Christians pursue lowliness, meekness, and long-suffering, they do not know the purpose for being lowly, meek, and long-suffering. Even the purpose of being lowly, meek, and long-suffering has become a mystery to them. This mystery is the church. God wants us to have lowliness, meekness, and long-suffering so that we can live out the church life.

The Church Life Being a Serious Test

Therefore, God's intention is for Christ to be our life so that we can have the church as our living. God's desire is that our life would be entirely Christ so that what we live out would be entirely the church. If we have such a vision, in everything we do we will ask ourselves, "In doing this particular work, am I living out the church or something of myself? In being so careful to avoid any problem, am I doing this so that my self will be preserved whole or so that the church will be perfected? Am I reading the Word, praying, pursuing, laboring, and serving for my own spirituality or for the building up of the church?" Questions of this kind are a great test. Some only care for their own spirituality rather than for the church life even in their prayers and pursuits. This is due to their lack of such a vision, their not knowing such a mystery.

If a person truly has seen God's vision, immediately he will realize that God's intention is not to build up individual spirituality but to build up the church as the Body of Christ. Hence, he will sacrifice and put aside everything that damages the church, regardless of how good it is, including his own spirituality. Therefore, the vision of this mystery is the solution to all the questions. If you were to ask me, "Is it all right for me to go to a certain place to preach the gospel?" My answer would be: "When you go to preach the gospel, will the church there be built up or destroyed?" I know some will say, "Oh, I do not care about this. As long as people are saved, it is good enough." Please remember, however, that this is not sufficient. Of course, under normal circumstances, people being saved and the church being built up are one and the same thing. The condition today, however, is abnormal. Some of the work of preaching the gospel to save souls not only does not build up the church but actually tears down the building, the oneness, of the church. This is an extremely abnormal situation. Therefore, under the present circumstances, it is not enough just to ask whether people are being saved; we also have to ask whether the church is being built up. The principle is the same when we help others to pursue spirituality. Under normal circumstances, the pursuit of spirituality builds up the church, but today the situation is rather abnormal. Many pay attention to seeking spirituality, yet they tear down the building of the church. The reason that this happens is that they do not see the vision of God's mystery. This is a very solemn test to us.

Now I would like to give you some of my personal testimony. I was tested numerous times. In the past there were many good things that I did, things which seemed to others to be very profitable, yet within me I had a question: "If I do this, how will it affect the church?" Often when I asked myself this question, I could not do what I was doing anymore. Because I was under the restriction of the vision of the church, I had to give up many things that were seemingly good. Today I thank and praise the Lord. I have not regretted this one bit. Instead, I worship the Lord. I can testify that the church is not only a test but also a protection and a safeguard. If you pay attention only to whether a certain matter is good and beneficial, and you neglect the church, in the end you will have regret. However, if you care for the building of the church and sacrifice any other thing, even if it seems good and beneficial in your eyes, time will prove to you that God is with you.

WILLING TO BE TESTED AND RESTRICTED BY CHRIST AND THE CHURCH

Therefore, not only is Christ our test, but also the church is our test. Christ is a test to us to see whether or not we take Him as life and allow Him to live out through us. The church is a test to us to see whether the things we do are for the building up or the tearing down of the church. Both kinds of testing should always be with us. We should always ask ourselves: "Am I living by taking Christ as my life? Am I living by Christ or by my natural life?" Moreover, we should also ask: "Are my living, my walk, my service, and my work for the building up of the church or just for the sake of doing something good?"

May the Lord show us these two matters—Christ is our life and the church is our living. May Christ and the church become our vision, so that in everything we are restricted, tested, and directed, as well as delivered and preserved, by this vision. We cannot live by ourselves; instead, we should live by Christ, because Christ is our life. Moreover, we cannot live independently; rather, we must live in the church, because the church is our living.

Christ and the church are a great mystery, a mystery that we have seen from God for many years now. Today this vision is becoming clearer and clearer. We feel that aside from this we have nothing else to speak and preach. What we preach and speak is just Christ and the church. May the Lord have mercy upon us that we may live in such a vision!

ABOUT THE AUTHOR

Witness Lee was born in 1905 in northern China and raised in a Christian family. At age 19 he was fully captured for Christ and immediately consecrated himself to preach the gospel for the rest of his life. Early in his service, he met Watchman Nee, a renowned preacher, teacher, and writer. Witness Lee labored together with Watchman Nee under his direction. In 1934 Watchman Nee entrusted Witness Lee with the responsibility for his publication operation, called the Shanghai Gospel Bookroom.

Prior to the Communist takeover in 1949, Witness Lee was sent by Watchman Nee and his other co-workers to Taiwan to insure that the things delivered to them by the Lord would not be lost. Watchman Nee instructed Witness Lee to continue the former's publishing operation abroad as the Taiwan Gospel Bookroom, which has been publicly recognized as the publisher of Watchman Nee's works outside China. Witness Lee's work in Taiwan manifested the Lord's abundant blessing. From a mere 350 believers, newly fled from the mainland, the churches in Taiwan grew to 20,000 in five years.

In 1962 Witness Lee felt led of the Lord to come to the United States, settling in California. During his 35 years of service in the U.S., he ministered in weekly meetings and weekend conferences, delivering several thousand spoken messages. Much of his speaking has since been published as over 400 titles. Many of these have been translated into over fourteen languages. He gave his last public conference in February 1997 at the age of 91.

He leaves behind a prolific presentation of the truth in the Bible. His major work, *Life-study of the Bible,* comprises over 25,000 pages of commentary on every book of the Bible from the perspective of the believers' enjoyment and experience of God's divine life in Christ through the Holy Spirit. Witness Lee was the chief editor of a new translation of the New Testament into Chinese called the Recovery Version and directed the translation of the same into English. The Recovery Version also appears in a number of other languages. He provided an extensive body of footnotes, outlines, and spiritual cross references. A radio broadcast of his messages can be heard on Christian radio stations in the United States. In 1965 Witness Lee founded Living Stream Ministry, a non-profit corporation, located in Anaheim, California, which officially presents his and Watchman Nee's ministry.

Witness Lee's ministry emphasizes the experience of Christ as life and the practical oneness of the believers as the Body of Christ. Stressing the importance of attending to both these matters, he led the churches under his care to grow in Christian life and function. He was unbending in his conviction that God's goal is not narrow sectarianism but the Body of Christ. In time, believers began to meet simply as the church in their localities in response to this conviction. In recent years a number of new churches have been raised up in Russia and in many eastern European countries.

OTHER BOOKS PUBLISHED BY
Living Stream Ministry

Titles by Witness Lee:

Title	ISBN
Abraham—Called by God	0-7363-0359-6
The Experience of Life	0-87083-417-7
The Knowledge of Life	0-87083-419-3
The Tree of Life	0-87083-300-6
The Economy of God	0-87083-415-0
The Divine Economy	0-87083-268-9
God's New Testament Economy	0-87083-199-2
The World Situation and God's Move	0-87083-092-9
Christ vs. Religion	0-87083-010-4
The All-inclusive Christ	0-87083-020-1
Gospel Outlines	0-87083-039-2
Character	0-87083-322-7
The Secret of Experiencing Christ	0-87083-227-1
The Life and Way for the Practice of the Church Life	0-87083-785-0
The Basic Revelation in the Holy Scriptures	0-87083-105-4
The Crucial Revelation of Life in the Scriptures	0-87083-372-3
The Spirit with Our Spirit	0-87083-798-2
Christ as the Reality	0-87083-047-3
The Central Line of the Divine Revelation	0-87083-960-8
The Full Knowledge of the Word of God	0-87083-289-1
Watchman Nee—A Seer of the Divine Revelation ...	0-87083-625-0

Titles by Watchman Nee:

Title	ISBN
How to Study the Bible	0-7363-0407-X
God's Overcomers	0-7363-0433-9
The New Covenant	0-7363-0088-0
The Spiritual Man 3 volumes	0-7363-0269-7
Authority and Submission	0-7363-0185-2
The Overcoming Life	1-57593-817-0
The Glorious Church	0-87083-745-1
The Prayer Ministry of the Church	0-87083-860-1
The Breaking of the Outer Man and the Release ...	1-57593-955-X
The Mystery of Christ	1-57593-954-1
The God of Abraham, Isaac, and Jacob	0-87083-932-2
The Song of Songs	0-87083-872-5
The Gospel of God 2 volumes	1-57593-953-3
The Normal Christian Church Life	0-87083-027-9
The Character of the Lord's Worker	1-57593-322-5
The Normal Christian Faith	0-87083-748-6
Watchman Nee's Testimony	0-87083-051-1

Available at
Christian bookstores, or contact Living Stream Ministry
2431 W. La Palma Ave. • Anaheim, CA 92801
1-800-549-5164 • www.livingstream.com